COLLEGE ADMISSIONS:

The Guidebook and Workbook for High School Students on Getting into College

Written by,

Kat McKay, J.D.

COLLEGE ADMISSIONS:

The Guidebook and Workbook for High School Students on Getting into College

Table of Contents:

The College Admissions Guidebook

The College Admissions Workbook

The College Admissions Guidebook

Introduction

This guidebook discusses what you should do during your years of high school to prepare to apply to college. It is arranged in four chapters; each chapter is related to a grade level of high school. However, the book topics can be used during any year of high school. Therefore, the guidebook is also organized by subject matter. Simply check the table of contents, and flip to the subject in which you are interested to use this book without relation to grade level. Overall, the guidebook seeks to prepare you to apply to colleges and universities as a high school senior.

A note regarding the word "college": As a high school senior, you will apply for admission to attend a school of higher education and work toward an undergraduate degree (usually a Bachelor of Arts or a Bachelor of Science degree). Colleges are generally institutions of higher education granting undergraduate degrees, and universities are generally institutions of higher education granting both undergraduate degrees and graduate degrees. This book will use the terms interchangeably, and you will likely apply to both types of schools.

The College Admissions Guidebook

Chapter One

This chapter will cover what to do in the ninth grade year to best prepare for admission to colleges and universities.

Part One: Course Selection Basics

Graduation from high school is a prerequisite to entering college. A prerequisite is a requirement that you must complete before taking the next step. It is usually used in the context of coursework. For example, you must complete the course German Language I with a passing grade before you may take German Language II. Here we are going to consider how to best structure your high school coursework in a way that ensures that you graduate on time and in a way that positions you in the best possible way to be admitted to college when you apply near the end of your high school years.

Colleges consider your grades and the courses in which you received your grades. Upon entering high school, a significant question should be "what classes should I register for this year?" Every year (or every semester if your high school schedules classes twice per year), you should ask yourself this question.

This chapter is going to provide an initial roadmap for course selection in the ninth grade, and every year in high school, you may consider refining your initial plan (which you originally made in the ninth grade) for additional tailoring to that later year. If you are not a ninth grade student (maybe you have begun this book later in your high school career), then start your roadmap now as well. It is better to create a plan later than not to create one at all, and doing so will improve your chances of college admission.

Remember our original prerequisite? It was, and continues to be, graduation from high school. Let us structure our plan with that as our constant guidepost and with college admission and enrollment upon graduation as our ultimate destination. We will move forward with the following delineated steps, helping us to advance toward college.

Step one is to obtain the list of requirements for graduation from your high school guidance counselor's office. This document (it might be a packet, pamphlet, or small paper bound book) will list graduation requirements, such as the number of math, science, language arts, social studies, and foreign language courses that you must take. I call these five course areas the main subject areas. While high schools often only consider four subject areas to be the core areas (math, science, language arts, and social studies), I believe that foreign language (especially a significant amount of one foreign language) will assist with your college admission, provided your grades are good. Therefore, foreign language should be considered a main subject area (or core area). These five course types are the courses that are most important for colleges to see on your transcript (this is the document that your high school prepares showing the courses you have taken, and the grades you have received in them; you will submit it with your college applications). They are also the most important course areas in which colleges will want you to achieve good grades.

Your list of graduation requirements will delineate the courses you must take. For example, within a math requirement that requires four math courses, you may have a requirement of algebra and a requirement of geometry—both of which must be taken. Your list of requirements will also delineate those courses you can choose and which will count toward the number of credits you need to graduate. For example, if your math requirement is four courses, and two must be algebra and geometry, you may choose the other two from the list of math courses that will count toward your graduation requirement, but which are not specified by name.

Over four years of high school for a math requirement such as the requirement in our above example, you would take: four math courses including: (1) algebra; (2) geometry; (3) a math course from the approved math requirement list, which is your choice; and (4) a second math course from the approved math requirement list, which is your choice. The school would also allow you to take additional math courses as elective courses. You may take additional math courses, but you may not take fewer math courses.

The other main subject areas will also follow this format for course selection. Each high school has different course requirements. Therefore, your requirements will differ from the examples in this book, so make sure you always follow the specific requirements of your high school. For example, many high schools have requirements for the number of years of foreign language that you must take to graduate. They may have music, physical education, health, and other course requirements that you also need to factor into your schedule.

Step two is to obtain the current list of courses offered by your high school this semester. This can also be found in the counselor's office. You will want the current list of courses that are being offered in the upcoming semester and as far in the future as the school has available. The list may be a large list applicable to all students, or it may be organized by grade level (portions of it may be applicable only to specific grade levels). It may also vary by semester. For example, German Language I may be offered every fall semester, but not in the spring semesters (when German Language II is only offered instead).

Because of changes to the list over time, explain to the counselor (or personnel in the main office of your high school) that you need a list of courses offered for the entire year. If only the fall semester list is available, then ask for a list showing the courses usually offered in the spring (such as the spring course list from the last year). If your school changes the course list according to grade level, then ask for the lists for all four grade levels. Having this information will enable you to create a master course plan for yourself, which you will then re-evaluate every year.

Feel comfortable asking for, and explaining why, you need the list of requirements for graduation from your high school and the list of courses offered by your high school to the counselor or any high school personnel. People who work in schools (such as counselors, secretaries, and others with whom you may speak outside of the classroom) love to hear that you are thinking ahead to college. They want you to ensure that you fulfill all of the requirements for graduation and position yourself well for college admissions.

Positioning yourself well for college admissions means that you have put yourself into the best possible position for acceptance by selecting the best courses, having a good grade point average, engaging in appropriate extracurricular activities, achieving your best SAT or ACT score, and drafting an excellent college application.

Step three is to create a course selection plan. Once you have your two lists (steps one and two), and you know the basics regarding how these lists will work (such as our math example of four courses required, with two being specific requirements and two being your choice), we will discuss how to create a course selection plan. To start yours, take a full sheet of paper and make the following list, or fill in the example charts that go with this book:

Ninth Grade Fall Semester

Math

Science

Language arts

Social studies

Foreign language

Sixth course

Seventh course (provided your school has a seventh period)

Ninth Grade Spring Semester

Math

Science

Language arts

Social studies

Foreign language

Sixth course

Seventh course (provided your school has a seventh period)

To fill in the plan that you have written (or the chart that goes with this book), you will write the course you will take in each listed subject area that will fulfill a graduation requirement. First, determine the number of courses that you will need to complete to graduate from high school. Your high school might use the term "credits." This is often used in college, and it means that some courses are worth more than other courses when they are applied toward your graduation requirements. A one-credit course is worth only a small amount toward graduation (one credit), and a three-credit course is worth three times as much toward meeting your graduation requirements (three credits). For example, if your school requires fifteen credits per semester for four years to graduate, it requires thirty total credits per year: fifteen in the fall and fifteen in the spring.

If you take one-credit courses, you will need to take additional course credits (which means additional courses) to earn the fifteen credits for that semester. Generally, courses worth fewer credits should take less time and be less intense or easier. However, sometimes this is not the case, and you might end up spending a great deal of time on a course that is not worth as much toward graduation.

Courses with more credits also count more toward your grade point average. An A in a course with three credits is worth three times as much on your transcript as an A in a course worth one credit.

Once you have determined the number of courses (or credits) that you will need each year to graduate, you must then determine the number of requirements needed to graduate. For example, I need six courses per semester (a total of twelve courses total per year) and forty-eight courses total over four years to graduate. (There is also a chart in the workbook that goes with this guidebook, which can help you to keep track of this information.)

Next, determine the number of courses that you will need to take in math, science, language arts, social studies, and foreign language as well as other required courses (such as health or gym) and enter it on the chart created for this book. Also, determine the specific courses you need to take within each subject area based on the graduation requirements, which you obtained from your high school, and

16

enter them on the chart for this book. For example, your high school's overall list might look like the example list below, but always note that every high school's list will vary. So, make sure you meet your school's specific graduation requirements.

The following information is a simplified version of what you are trying to learn when you read your high school course list, which will then help you to fill in your list for each academic year. You can enter this information on the chart created for this book.

Example List of Courses for a High School

In four years, I need to complete 48 classes. This means that I need to complete 12 classes per year (six classes per semester). For my school, the 48 classes must include:

Four math classes

> One must be algebra;
>
> One must be geometry; and
>
> Two I may choose from the math courses listed on the high school math course list. These must be taken in order (for example, Algebra II may only be allowed after Algebra I).

Four science classes

One must be biology;

One must be chemistry;

One must be either physics or physiology; and

One I may choose from the science courses listed on the high school science course list. Note that some science courses have a prerequisite. For example, biochemistry may only be allowed after chemistry is completed in your school (chemistry would be the prerequisite for biochemistry).

Five language arts classes

One must be an introductory literature course;

One must be an advanced literature course (which must be taken after the introductory literature course);

One must be an essay writing course or a creative writing course; and

Two I may choose from the language arts courses listed on the high school language arts course list.

Five social studies classes

One must be an American history course;

One must be an ancient history course;

One must be a course in current events; and

Two I may choose from the social studies courses listed on the high school social studies course list.

Two foreign language classes

These two courses must be in the same language and must be sequential courses (for example, German I followed by German II). Note, that the prerequisite for German II is German I. German I must come first. Also, German I and then French I will not complete this requirement.

One health class

I may choose from the high school health course list.

One physical education class

I may choose from the high school physical education course list.

One music class

I may choose band, orchestra, chorus, or music composition.

The remaining courses (to bring the student to the required 48 courses) are all elective classes. I may fill these with additional courses from the main subject areas, or I may choose from the elective course list.

Under our plan, the last one or two course spots (the sixth course and seventh course spots) are your choice (such as orchestra, band, or art). Start with non-academic requirements in those spots this year. For example, fill in any physical education requirement your school may have and any music requirement. Then once requirements are fulfilled, you will still have five courses from the main course areas, and two choice courses.

Always remember that you must plan your schedule to ensure that you take the lower-level courses early so that you can take the upper-level courses sequentially. For example, if chemistry is a prerequisite to biochemistry, then chemistry is the lower-level course that must be completed before you take biochemistry, which is the upper-level course.

Once you understand the number of courses (or credits) that you will need to take, how many are in each subject, and the required course types under each header, then fill in the plan that you have written (or the chart created for this book) titled "Ninth Grade Fall Semester" and "Ninth Grade Spring Semester." To do this, you will write the course that you plan to take in each listed subject area. Try to fulfill a specific course graduation requirement with each spot. This is an example of a completed ninth grade schedule based on our example high school's requirements (below). You can fill in the chart created for this book to write down and organize this information easily.

Ninth Grade Fall Semester (Example)

Math – required algebra

Science – required biology

Language arts – required introductory literature (this must be completed before advanced literature)

Social studies – required American history

Foreign language – German I (this must be completed before German II)

Sixth course – orchestra (this fulfills the music requirement)

Seventh course (provided your school has a seventh period) – physical education (this fulfills the physical education requirement)

Ninth Grade Spring Semester (Example)

Math – required geometry

Science – required chemistry

Language arts – required advanced literature

Social studies – a required social studies course from the

approved list (because neither ancient history nor current

events were offered this semester)

Foreign language – German II

Sixth course – orchestra

Seventh course (provided your school has a seventh period) –

health (this fulfills the health requirement)

For your fourth step, double check your list and ask

your guidance counselor or parent to ensure that you have

correctly understood the required courses for your school

(based on your school's requirements as shown in the

information, which you obtained from your school). If you

have, it is now time to further discuss strategy for course

selection. We will next discuss why to select certain courses

rather than how courses are selected based on graduation

requirements (which we have just done).

Part Two: Course Selection Strategy

In this section, I will further discuss the strategy that I recommend you follow for course selection in high school. It will outline the entire four-year strategy for you as well as describe why you should select courses this way in the ninth grade. If you understand the strategy as a whole, you will be likely to adopt it and begin now.

In the ninth grade, take required courses in all five main subject areas (math, science, language arts, social studies, and foreign language) for both semesters. Exposure to these ten courses will help you to learn the main subject areas in which your talents lie and whether you enjoy them as well. In

23

addition, you will complete a significant number of high school requirements. Finally, academic courses are the courses that college admissions personnel believe are the most important.

At the close of these ten courses, taken over two semesters, you will know your current talents. If you are talented in language arts, social studies, and foreign language, then you will know that you should likely take two semesters of each of these courses for the entire four years of high school. You will have achieved eight semesters of the main subject area courses in which you excel by graduation. You will appear to be someone who is a hard worker and to be someone with direction.

Every student is talented in several areas. Students in high school should recognize that your best courses are the ones in which you are talented. If you have B's in your best courses (or B– or occasional C+ grades in these courses), then you can consider yourself to be talented in them if you do better in them than you do in the other main subject areas. It is easier to get into college with excellent grades; however, you need to take main subject area courses as well. Therefore, you will pick the ones in which you do the best, require yourself to put in significant effort, and consider those your ever-improving talents.

You choose the three main subject areas in which you are the most talented, meaning that your grades in these subjects are better than the other two main subject areas for which you have taken introductory courses (in our example, these are science and math).

The main point is that you will continue to have seven (in some schools, six) hours per day, and five hours will always be in main subject areas. However, you will eventually transition from having each main subject area for one period per day to letting go of up to two main subject areas after those requirements are fulfilled. In those two places, you will add in additional courses in the main subject areas in which you excel. A specific example will help to clarify the idea. The ninth grade fall example looked like this:

Ninth Grade Fall Semester (Example)

Math – required algebra

Science – required biology

Language arts – required introductory literature (this must be completed before advanced literature)

Social studies – required American history

Foreign language – German I (this must be completed before German II)

Sixth course – orchestra (this fulfills the music requirement)

Seventh course (provided your school has a seventh period) – physical education (this fulfills the physical education requirement)

An example of the same student's course selection in eleventh grade, after all of the main subject area requirements have been completed, could be very different. The student may choose those main subject areas that the student wishes to let go of once those requirements are completed. Therefore, eleventh grade might look like this instead:

Eleventh Grade Fall Semester (Example)

Language arts – a literature course

Language arts – an essay writing course

Social studies – a history course

Foreign language – German V

Foreign language – French I

Sixth course – orchestra or another fun elective

Seventh course (provided your school has a seventh period) – a fun elective

Importantly, if you have an interest in continuing any main subject area, do so. For example, if you are best in math, language arts, and foreign language, but you hope someday to be a physician or a laboratory scientist, then you must certainly continue with science as well (you then have four main subject areas for eight semesters, and you remove only social studies when the high school requirements are completed). When you remove social studies, you will add in an extra course in any of the main subject areas that you have chosen to keep (you might take two science courses, math, language arts, and foreign language for the five main subject areas after letting go of social studies).

Eliminate up to two main subject areas only after the high school requirements are fully completed, and you know that you are ready to let go of the main subject areas. If you cannot do this because you are not sure of the direction in which you are headed ("I might want to be anything, the sky's the limit!"), then the answer is easy: take eight semesters of every main subject area (math, science, language arts, social studies, and foreign language). Also, use this plan if you attend a very small school without as many options from which to choose courses. Always take five courses in main subject areas.

If you plan to apply for a specialized program in a college such as music, dance, fine arts, or theater, then make sure that your two elective spots (your sixth and seventh course hours) are dedicated to your specialized field of interest. For example, if you would like to be a professional violinist, make sure that you take eight semesters of orchestra (the sixth course period) and eight semesters of any other courses your school offers which might be related to your musical goal (the seventh course period). Five courses in the main subject areas will not preclude you from taking the additional courses that are geared toward your specialized collegiate goal. If your school has seven hours, then you have two extra course spots. If it has six hours, then you have one extra spot.

Remember, when allocating the main subject area spots (five courses on your schedule), you can remove two main subject areas and replace those courses with additional courses in the main subject areas in which you are the most talented. Do this, *only* after: (1) the high school requirements are fulfilled for your school; and (2) you know that you are ready to make the choice to concentrate on the remaining main subject areas in which you are talented.

Once you make the transition to allocating your five academic course spots to the main subject areas in which your talents lie, then your grades in these subjects will be better than the other introductory courses. This will immediately bring up your grade point average by letting go of the courses in which you have lower grades and adding in their places courses in which you have higher grades. For example, if you had a B+ in math and a C in language arts, when you let go of language arts and add a math course in its place, you will be more likely to have two B+'s that semester than if you kept language arts. Additionally, because you take so many of the same types of courses after the transition, you will start to get really good at them, increasing your grade point average in the later years of high school. Taking two math courses per semester might bring up those two B+'s to two A-'s in later courses.

Each year of math will prepare you for more difficult math; it will also put you into a select pool of students who are applying to college with over eight semesters of math (more than four full years). You will be in that select pool of students because in some semesters you are doubling up on math courses. The same is true for students who add in a second foreign language. If you plan to have eight semesters of German, then you drop a different main subject area and you add in French, you will be in a select pool of college applicants who have eight semesters of one language (German) and maybe four of another (French). This impresses college admissions personnel.

Consider it this way: for a student concentrating on language arts courses (and letting go of math instead) your language arts class on grammar will result in better writing. The literature courses will result in essays that are more creative. These additional language arts skills will help you to achieve better grades. These courses will also help with classes that have other writing requirements, enabling you to write a better term paper for a social studies course, for example.

Starting this course selection strategy now will help you to:

(1) Fulfill your high school's course requirements for graduation early;

(2) Identify the main subject areas in which your talents lie while you still have time to take extra semesters of courses in those subjects. It would be a shame to learn that you are good at foreign language in your junior year of high school when you can only take four semesters of it before college. It would have been much better to start freshman year so you could showcase eight semesters on your transcript.

(3) Identify the main subject areas in which you are not so good. If your grades suffer in a required course area, such as math, then take the required semesters in your freshman and sophomore years. It is better to get requirements out of the way early when you are not good at them. This is because the later two years of high school can include courses in main subject areas in which you are talented. Your grade point average will increase when the math is completed at the end of sophomore year. You will be able to show college

admissions personnel that you have increased your grade point average and that you have direction in your course of study.

Completing required courses as early as possible in your high school career means that you have time during the later years to take more courses in the subjects in which you are talented. You can position yourself as dedicated and hardworking, and can show that you are able to increase your grade point average over time. (Advanced Placement Courses and Exams will be discussed in this book in sections related to later high school years.)

If you are concerned about taking five courses in the main subject areas at the same time, I suggest that you ask your guidance counselor to register you for easier versions of the main subject area courses (and confirm that the easier course will also fulfill the requirement). Do this for courses in the main subject areas for which you have not fulfilled the high school requirement and those subject areas where you achieve lower grades (or in ninth grade, when you anticipate that this is an area of weakness for you).

For example, if you are worried about math, then ask for guidance regarding which math courses are easier. Confirm that the recommended easier course will also fulfill your high school's math requirement.

If it is language that concerns you, then ask the guidance counselor which teachers or languages are easier to stick with for students attending your school. For example, ask whether Spanish teachers keep students for eight successful semesters more often than French teachers. There might be a reason that more students take four years of this language, while more students transfer out of another language.

Tell the guidance counselor your plan very openly and honestly. Tell him or her that you would like to fulfill requirements to see in which subjects your talents lie, and that these courses (in our example, math and language) are the subjects about which you are nervous. Therefore, you want to register for courses in which you can succeed (which in math or language might be easier versions of the course or teachers who are more inclined to grade easily).

Part Three: Good Grade Basics

Our strategy regarding course selection is to first complete required courses by taking courses in each of the five main subject areas. Then, tailor your schedule to encompass additional courses in the three main subject areas in which you are talented, while you allow yourself to remove the courses from up to two areas in which you are not successful. Each part of the strategy involves five main subject area courses to be taken for all four years and for electives (or specialized courses such as band) to fill up the remaining course openings (your school may allow six or seven courses to be taken.)

Keeping the great majority of your courses in the main subject areas is smart because these are the subject areas college admissions personnel will most want to see on your transcript. (Remember, a transcript is the document that your high school prepares listing the courses you have taken, and the grades you have received, in each course.) You will submit your transcript with your college applications. College admissions personnel want to see both the main subject area courses on your transcript as well as good grades in as many courses as possible. The transcript lists grades for each course (German I: A) and gives a number for all of your courses averaged together. The grade point average is on a 4.0 scale for most schools. This means that an A average is a 4.0; a B average is a 3.0; a C average is a 2.0, and numbers in between are used to show the specific average for that student. For example, your grade point average might be 3.25, which is slightly lower than a B+. Grades in advanced placement courses affect grade point averages differently (for example, a B in an advanced placement course may be worth more than a regular course on your transcript. It may be worth 4.0, which is an A in other courses).

This section will discuss how to maximize your grade point average while taking courses from the main subject areas and how this plan of course selection can also help you to improve your grade point average in the later years of high school (which will show admissions personnel that your grades improved over the high school years).

You will want a strong grade point average in solid courses. Aiming for the main subject areas ensures solid courses play the most significant role on your transcript for all four years of high school. Transitioning to courses in the main subject areas in which you find your strengths will help you to increase your grade point average while keeping solid coursework on your transcript. It will also allow you to take the main subject area courses that you prefer. Most students have better experiences in courses in which they do well, and enjoying a course often motivates a student to perform well.

Hopefully, your grade point average and course enjoyment increase when you get to take more courses in the main subject areas in which you are successful and fewer in the subject areas that are more of a struggle.

This transition occurs when, to use our example from earlier in the book, if you had a B+ in math and a C in language arts, when you let go of language arts and add a math course in its place, you will be more likely to have two B+'s that semester then if you had kept language arts.

There are even more ways that taking the same types of courses can increase your opportunities to increase your grade point average. First, taking courses in the same subject areas (rather than many varied areas) can help you to develop excellent study skills specifically geared toward success in that type of course.

Also, knowledge from one course will begin to help you do better work in similar courses. For example, if you take more social studies than most other students, knowledge of historical time periods will help you in other courses that have a large historical component. That knowledge will also help you in social studies courses dealing with current events. For example, knowing how our government was initially structured can help you to see how it has changed, or knowledge about various wars that occurred in the past can help you to discuss modern day world conflicts with increased understanding.

You will also be able to better identify those teachers with prior courses in which you excelled, and register for other courses they teach. Sticking with teachers who motivate you and who appreciate your work can also increase your grade point average and your course enjoyment.

Additionally, because you take so many of the same types of courses after the transition, you will start to get really good at them, further increasing your grade point average in the later years of high school.

Part Four: Studying

Success in any course you take requires studying and dedication. Positivity will help you to dedicate your efforts to the course. It is now time to create a plan for studying. The main component of any study plan is dedicating time to studying. Committing two hours, per day, every day, to studying will increase your grade point average. Therefore, it will increase your success with college admissions.

I suggest that you start with a table or a desk that is free of clutter. Keep a basket next to the table or desk. When you sit down to study, if your desk is not an open, empty space, place anything on top quickly into the basket (a laundry basket will work). This ensures that you always have an uncluttered space to work and that you do not spend study time cleaning and organizing. Next, make a stack of your course books and notebooks on the desk (take them from your backpack). I like to put the homework that I usually like to do the most at the bottom of the stack and build up to the top of the stack, having the homework that I usually like to do the least. If you do this, you will begin with the homework that you like the least, and as the study session continues, it becomes more fun. For me, the last project to complete would likely be my favorite, which would be lengthy reading (especially for book reports), and for this, I would move to a soft chair for that final assignment.

A benefit of devoting two hours per day every day is allowing yourself to have a consistent schedule that is easier to plan. This is because studying ahead on nights that you do not have as much allows you to even out the nights that you would ordinarily have too much.

If you finish the homework and have time left in your study session, I recommend that you review what you have already done in the course up to that point (do this by re-reading your class notes and corrected homework). This is how you study for quizzes and tests in advance. This will certainly increase your course knowledge and grade point average. You will do better on pop quizzes and will avoid cramming for a test in one course while getting behind in another course.

For some courses, you can move ahead with homework or get a head start on reports. For example, if you have a book report that will be due in a month, then read ahead (and write the report ahead of time too). This enables you to even out the hours that you will spend later. There will also rarely be a last minute rush to complete the project. Rushing and cramming at the end of a project for one course can sometimes harm steady progress in other courses because you might get behind in them.

Discussing assignments early with your teacher (such as, asking if your chosen book will work for the next book report or if your paper topic is satisfactory) will show your teacher that you are committed to your coursework and getting a good grade in that course. Showing a high level of commitment to your teachers will help you to reach and maintain a higher grade point average.

Teachers want students to apply themselves and pay attention in class. Not only does paying attention and applying yourself improve your work, showing your teacher that you are doing so keys the teacher in to the idea that you are a committed and good student. Doing the work well is important and showing the teacher that you care will give you a good reputation among the teachers in your school. A fact that most ninth graders do not know is that if several teachers think that you are a good student, they will tell other teachers that you are a good student (in meetings, ninth grade teachers discuss ninth graders, tenth grade teachers discuss tenth graders, etc.). Your good reputation among the teachers will help you to get good grades in classes with other teachers.

Part Five: Working with a Tutor

Another way to improve your grade point average in the ninth grade (and in later years) is to obtain tutoring. There are two types of courses for which you will want to obtain tutoring: those that are a struggle, and those that are easy.

In the ninth grade, you will take courses in every main subject area. Working with a tutor will help you to achieve and maintain a higher grade point average in subjects in which you are struggling by helping you to keep a higher grade in a specific main subject area until you complete your high school's requirement for that main subject area. This will help keep your grade point average higher overall.

Obtaining tutoring in a subject area in which you struggle will also help you to become proficient in or, even good, at that subject. If your skills improve enough, the subject area can turn into a success and remain a main subject area, which you will want to take for eight semesters. Improving your skills in an area can enable you to keep up your grade point average while continuing to take courses in that area. By doing well in more main subject areas, you will broaden the range of collegiate programs to which you can successfully become admitted.

If you want to apply to college as a biology major (potentially aiming to go to medical school upon college graduation), then you will need to be successful in high school science, and you should take a lot of science courses. If this is your goal, then you will have to keep science as a main subject area in high school and keep your grade point average high. This is an area for which tutoring is a great option. Once you have a good grade point average in this area, keep up the tutoring to keep up your grade point average.

A great thing about tutoring is that it takes a student to a higher level of improvement, which he or she cannot always do through self-study. A student can increase skills and knowledge in a harder area, and by doing so, increase his or her college admissions potential in that area.

Subjects in which you feel that you are falling behind, or in which you have already fallen behind, are also great courses for which to seek out tutoring. For example, math is often based on how to complete or solve the prior step properly. If the class is moving forward faster than you are, or you need more practice to stay up to speed, then this is a time to call the tutoring center.

Language tutoring can also help you to succeed in those courses. For example, tutoring in language over the summer months can bring you back to school in the fall several steps ahead of the course. This can mean that a course you had trouble in last year can be a true success this year. Tutoring will help you to develop your talents.

Tutoring can also work for subjects that you are good in already. It can help you to stay on track and stay dedicated through increased accountability for spending time studying outside of school hours.

Setting aside time and creating a dedicated space for studying is crucially important. Once you have done this, a tutor can also help you to create study skills that will work for you. Tutors are experts in helping students to succeed and can help you to learn effective strategies for studying. They can guide you to books as well, which you can use to identify strategies for successful improvement (such as the course selection strategy, grade point average, and study strategies set forth in this book).

The College Admissions Guidebook

Chapter Two

This chapter will cover what to do in the tenth grade as you prepare for college admission. Specifically, it will discuss three important aspects of the tenth grade that can differ from the ninth grade and how to handle them successfully to improve your chances for college admissions.

Part One: Advanced Placement Courses and Exams

The "College Board" is a group of educators who oversee Advanced Placement Courses and Advanced Placement Exams. These are often called "AP Courses" and "AP Exams" or "APs." Advanced Placement Courses are courses that your school may offer (and likely will offer) that are considered to be college-level courses. There are many types of AP courses, such as Advanced Placement World History, Advanced Placement Chemistry, Advanced Placement English Literature and Composition, and Advanced Placement German Language and Culture. These are only some examples of the Advanced Placement courses offered in various schools.

Advanced Placement Courses are more challenging than standard high school courses, but if you pass the course with a good grade, it will look excellent on your high school transcript. Often, a grade of a B (usually a 3.0) in an Advanced Placement Course will be reflected as an A (which is a 4.0) on your high school transcript. Different schools offer different Advanced Placement Courses and handle the grading on the transcripts in a way that is consistent with the grading scale of the school. For example, the grading is different for schools that use a different grading scale, and some schools handle Advanced Placement Course grading in other ways. No matter how your school handles the grading, it remains that by doing well in an Advanced Placement Course, your transcript reflects that you took a college-level course.

Upon successful completion of the Advanced Placement Course, your transcript will reflect the completion of the Advanced Placement Course, and it also will likely contain the "bump up" in the grade that you received. Sometimes your transcript will reflect the letter grade for the course (in our example, a B) with the numerical value having the "bump up," which is often an entire point difference on a 4.0 scale. A B is usually given the value of 3.0, but the Advanced Placement Course B can be given the value of 4.0. This then increases your grade point average as though you received an A in the course. The reason many high schools do this is to provide an increased grade point average for students who take college-level courses in high school (the college-level courses are the Advanced Placement Courses).

Each Advanced Placement Course culminates with an Advanced Placement Exam (usually in mid-May). The Advanced Placement Exam is taken by the students who took the course (with some exceptions for home-schooled students and others who may also take the exam). It is given under strict test conditions, usually also at the high school which you attend and where you took the course. However, the Advanced Placement Exams may be administered by two schools together and sometimes non-school facilities are used as test sites. If you want to take an Advanced Placement Course and an Advanced Placement Exam that is not offered by your school, then speak with your high school guidance counselor, and he or she will guide you. You may also visit the official Advanced Placement website, which is set up by the College Board. (The College Board is the group of educators that administer the Advanced Placement program with high schools and colleges.)

A student who does well on the exam may earn college credit for the Advanced Placement Course. This means that because you have taken Advanced Placement World History, for example, and achieved a sufficiently good grade and exam score, you may be deemed, upon entry into college, to have fulfilled part of your college credit requirement. Always check with the colleges to which you are applying to determine their policies for Advanced Placement Course credits. These vary from college to college, but most colleges and universities have written policies that are available on their websites.

Advanced Placement Courses are often taken in the eleventh and twelfth grades, but they can be taken earlier. The College Board states that academically prepared tenth grade students can take them. If you decide that you would like to take an Advanced Placement Course in a specific subject (or several Advanced Placement Courses in several subjects), then you want to be prepared academically to take the course. Consider Advanced Placement Courses to be advanced courses that will be more challenging than other courses you take in high school. Also, remember that you will have an important Advanced Placement Exam in the spring following the course, which will require significant knowledge and study time. Then, ask your guidance counselor if you can register for the course that you would like to take. He or she will inform you whether the guidance office can enroll you itself or if you need a specific teacher's recommendation (or a specific preliminary course) at your school. This is a good thing to do early in the tenth grade year so that you are prepared to take the course as soon as possible, most likely in the eleventh grade year.

Preparation to take Advanced Placement Courses works right alongside the course selection roadmap recommended in the chapter of this book for the ninth grade year. By taking academic courses and concentrating your efforts on those subject areas in which your talents lie, you will take more of those courses. By doing so, you will develop a deeper knowledge of those subjects and be more prepared for Advanced Placement Courses in those subject areas.

You will want to take Advanced Placement Courses when you think you can do fairly well in them. Do not omit Advanced Placement Courses from consideration because you are not a perfect student. Students are people and people are not perfect. Do consider taking Advanced Placement Courses in the subject areas in which you concentrate much of your academic coursework. If you tend to take many science courses, then start to consider which Advanced Placement science courses it makes sense for you to take.

Also, communicate your interest in the Advanced Placement Courses, which you have identified for yourself, to your guidance counselor. Confirm that he or she will register you for the class and ask about any additional requirements that your school may have for enrolling in the Advanced Placement Course and taking the Advanced Placement Exam.

Advanced Placement Exam week is designated ahead of time by the College Board. This is a consistent time for all high schools to give the Advanced Placement Exams (it is often in early to mid-May.) You will want to know when the Advanced Placement Exams will take place and mark your calendar. Also, Advanced Placement Exams cost money (which the College Board charges to your school), and most schools will require the student to pay the high school for the exam (so that the high school can reimburse the College Board). Students in public high schools usually have to pay something for the exam but can take the exam for free or at a lower cost if the student demonstrates financial need. You can discuss these topics with your guidance counselor.

The upside of taking Advanced Placement Courses and Advanced Placement Exams is also financial. By having an excellent high school transcript, you may become a candidate for more merit-based scholarship money. Also, earning college credits ahead of time means that you have fewer requirements to fulfill in college (provided your college of choice accepts Advanced Placement Credits). You start college with some completed courses, which means that you are more likely to graduate from college on time, or if you are very diligent, maybe a bit ahead of schedule.

Another benefit of taking Advanced Placement Courses is that you will experience courses near to college level while you prepare to enter college. By doing moderately well in these, you will gain confidence that you will succeed in college. Finally, work done in Advanced Placement Courses can be used to showcase your talents as a student. It is a good idea to set aside a few pieces of your best work each year so that you have these when you are looking to provide an example of your writing or another example of your excellent work. Examples of your best work might include creative and other writing samples, a written translation you did for a language class, or a summary of a science experiment that you performed and for which you kept a record.

Advanced Placement Courses provide great opportunities to create this work product, and then you have them when you need them during the college admissions process. Written work created in an Advanced Placement Course can be the basis of your college admissions essay. If you write on the topic of a college admissions essay (such as, a specific question asked on the application of one university to which you may apply) for a course project (such as, a course letting you write on a topic of your choice for a writing assignment), then you can use the coursework directly for your college applications. This is one way to involve a teacher in helping to show you the strengths of your essay and to suggest the edits and revisions which you should consider making.

Part Two: Extracurricular Activities as Preparation for Specialty Programs in Universities

When we think of extracurricular activities in high school, we think of the fact that they are fun, social, and enriching. They help high school students to explore who they are through the pursuit of non-academic activities and allow them to make similarly interested friends. College admissions personnel are generally only interested in extracurricular activities to the extent that they allow the admissions personnel to learn a little bit more about who the student is as a person. Extracurricular activities take up a great deal of time, energy, and devotion in high school, but they do not account for a significant part of the college admissions decisions for most schools. Academics are the main guiding factor for college admissions, with standardized admissions testing taking second place.

With that said, college admissions personnel will devote significant consideration to auditions (such as those for dance, theater, or music programs at the university), art portfolios, or other examples of your aptitude for, and experience in, particular fields that you wish to pursue as a student in college.

Specialty programs such as music, dance, theater, painting, and other fine arts, contain an overlap between academics and extracurricular pursuits. If you are seeking admission to an arts department in a college as a dancer, musician, actor, artist, or other such student, then extracurricular pursuits of this nature create experience that becomes important for admissions purposes. Time spent in theater performances or in dance troupes, music lessons, or art studios, takes on a new tenor (do not forget choral groups) when it is time to shine on your college applications.

To gain admission to these specialty programs, students should seek out experiences (inside and outside of school), which can provide the student with practice in his or her field of interest. For example, a flutist (a person who plays the flute) would want to join the school band and take private lessons. She would also want to keep examples of her work for college admissions purposes. For example, each time she reaches her full potential playing a solo musical composition, she should make a recording of it. She should note the recording with when she played it and how it exemplifies her abilities.

An actor should involve himself in high school theater productions and some outside of school acting lessons or performances, if possible. He should keep records of his performances and parts played, as well as making audio or video recordings, as he moves through high school. Keeping examples of work in genre appropriate formats also works for dance, painting, ceramics, and other arts (such as keeping paintings, portfolios, and pictures of your work and displays).

Outside of those students who are preparing for entry into these specialty collegiate programs, college admissions personnel like to see continuity in extracurricular pursuits. For example, four years of soccer could work well because for non-specialty programs (such as science majors), extracurricular pursuits are not significantly important to college admissions. Therefore, if you are not seeking to enter a specialty program, I suggest that you do things you like, have fun, and make friends. When it comes time to apply, phrase whatever it is you have enjoyed in the small space allocated to it on your application. Students are often surprised when they compare the time spent on extracurricular pursuits with how little it seems to matter to standard academic college admissions.

Part Three: Collegiate Athletics and Athletic Extracurricular Activities

If you plan to seek out collegiate athletics, then spend lots of time practicing your sport. However, stellar academics are much more likely to gain your admission to a good college than stellar sports performances. It is much more likely that you will gain admission to a school through academic performance. If you are well practiced in your sport, then you can identify schools that: (1) you are likely to become admitted to based on academic achievement; and (2) which you believe might be a school where you can make the team. For example, if you are a soccer player, you will want to identify schools that will likely accept you based on academics, as well as which you think have soccer teams that perform at your level of play. Then, you may be able to play your sport in college.

For many sports, you will try out for the team after you enroll as a student in the school. For those schools and sports programs, you first must become admitted academically. Next, you try out for the team. This is a process that involves a great deal of hope that you will make the team after enrolling in the school (enrolling means that you have applied, have been accepted for admission, and have officially decided to go to the school).

It is a good idea to confirm the process in your sport with the schools that you think you might want to attend. For example, if you play soccer and want to play in college, first identify the schools that will likely admit you based on academics. Second, see if the school has a soccer team at your level of play (by online review of sports statistics, team rankings, and maybe going to a game or a practice). Then, look up the email address of the coach(es) for the college teams that you are considering. Send a short and kind email to each coach stating that you play soccer and are hoping to play in college, very possibly for that coach and school. Ask the process by which students make that college's team. Also, ask if tryouts can be done prior to enrolling, or if they occur after enrolling in the college. This means that you are asking whether you can try out in your senior year of high school or if you can only try out after you are a student who attends the college already.

Most students of collegiate athletic teams are not "recruited." They try out after becoming admitted based on academic performance. If the coach and you communicate, he or she might want you for the team, and it could help you to make the team. However, most often, you are going to need to become admitted based on grades. Learning the process and timeframe for making the team at each school that you have identified for your sport is critical. The coach at each school can tell you the process. Keep all communications short and professional and do everything the coach asks of you. For example, if the coach says to contact a current student athlete at the school, or a team manager, then do so and ask that person questions. Do follow up and request the contact information of the person to which you are referred if the coach forgets to include it. Also, contact the coach again if that person to whom you were referred does not respond or cannot answer your questions.

This process (of contacting the coach) works well for smaller colleges and universities. Sometimes sports teams at these schools are also more accessible. Making the team for a large state university can sometimes be more difficult than making the team for a small college. However, this is not always the case. Seek out information on the level of play for the teams you are considering through team statistics, rankings, and by attending a practice or a game. Then, learn whether tryouts occur after enrollment and try to determine how many people do not make the team and how competitive tryouts usually are.

It is a tough fact that you might not make the team after you have already started school at the college and moved into the dormitories. When the college tryouts occur after enrollment, you have to accept the school without knowing if you will make the team. If you already go to the school and do not make the team, then you are still a student there. Therefore, apply to colleges knowing that you might not make the team. Make sure it is the right school for you academically. Then, you will have made a good decision even it if does not work out athletically.

Finally, a note on recruitment: we think of college "recruiters" as coming to a high school baseball game to observe a particular athlete. An initial question might be: "how was that athlete noticed in a way that brought the "recruiter" to the game?" Surprisingly, it is at times self-promotion to the coach or athletic department of the university that brings a representative of the university to observe your practice or game. Reaching out to the college with your amazing statistics can be an initial step to being noticed. It is not too different from emailing the coach about tryouts; you reach out with a short, professional email asking to be considered as a potential future player for that team. Then, in the email, provide your statistics on the ball field and ask about the process for playing for that college's team. The coach might explain the tryout process or might (on a very rare occasion) come and watch you play.

As a note, it is a good idea to learn the process for tryouts or recruitment at many schools. Send lots of emails, one to each potential school. Make each email specific to that coach and school. Keep them short and professional, and keep a good record, so you know that coach x is with school y, and you do not become confused about which coach (or athletic department secretary) has responded. Finally, it is a great idea to work on the email with your parents. However, it should come from your name. A coach likes to know that his or her student athletes are "go getters."

Finally, having your high school coach send the email can be tricky. They might not provide the attention to the initial email or the follow-ups that you will provide for yourself. Also, the high school coach may promote several players to the college coach at once (some of whom could outshine you on the field). It is likely best to leave the high school coach out of the conversation. If your high school coach also happens to promote you, then no harm is done. Most likely, you do not want your high school coach to determine with which colleges you communicate. You know your own academic status, and where you are likely to get in. Your coach may not promote you at all or to schools that are not academically appropriate for you.

Self-promoting is especially good for small colleges that you have personally identified as a good fit for you academically. A high school coach cannot promote every player to every college that player might attend. Do not put this time-consuming burden on them or burden yourself with having to go through them for permission for each email. Your future is your own.

Part Four: Behavioral Issues

The last note in the tenth grade chapter is one about behavioral issues in high school. Bad high school behavior can hinder college admissions. Do not skip classes and do not violate town curfews. Do not engage in any illegal activities whatsoever. These all have stark repercussions. Every disciplinary and legal record follows your academic career (and your career after college). Universities simply include a question about disciplinary and legal records on their applications. You do not want to have any bad behavior to report. It is the one answer on a college application for which you want no personal experience and nothing to communicate. Universities also confirm your answers and check on you with your high school. Additionally, police records can be disclosed to them by your town. Make sure to go to class and do only things that are legal and age appropriate. Getting into trouble can stop you from getting into college.

The College Admissions Guidebook

Chapter Three

This chapter will discuss what you should do in the eleventh grade to work toward getting into college. Including a review of your selected courses, considerations regarding where to apply to college, and studying for college admissions tests, including the American College Test (ACT) and Scholastic Aptitude Test (SAT). To refresh and keep your progress on track, the chapter also restates some key points regarding how to study and the benefits of keeping completed projects for use in college admissions applications.

Part One: Review Your Selected Courses

Before beginning the eleventh grade, re-check your academic course selection progress. First, review how many academic subjects you have taken in the ninth and tenth grades. Then, start to consider the colleges or universities to which you would possibly like to apply. Visit those schools' websites and check your courses against their guidelines for admissions. If the school recommends four years of particular courses for admissions purposes, then make sure to take four years of those courses. Schools often have suggested academic course guidelines for admissions purposes. A "unit," as listed on some schools' websites, may be a semester-long course, and for others, it may be a yearlong course. It is worth calling the school admissions office to ask whether a year of language arts (often termed "English" in college guidelines) is a "unit" or if a semester of language arts is a "unit." Keep in mind that most schools do not have specific admission requirements based on courses taken, but they will still list recommended courses (such as two "units" of science with lab use). Overall, this means that they are seeking high school students with transcripts reflecting both academic subject-matter courses (sometimes recommending the number of years or semesters of each such course), such as three "units" of math and good grades.

The recommended number of "units" (years or semesters) of foreign language or social studies is often just a recommendation. Try to meet, or come close to meeting, the course "unit" recommendations. However, if you reach the fall of your senior year and have fallen short of the course "unit" recommendations for a given school, then apply anyway. A guideline is not a hard and fast rule, and you have a transcript strong in academic courses. Many students apply even though they do not meet the course "unit" guidelines for various schools and many get in.

There is a balance between meeting recommended guidelines for courses taken and having a strong grade point average in the courses you choose. Many schools take their recommended course guidelines to be less important than a strong grade point average.

Another option is to apply to the school for admission under a different major. You can sometimes fulfill recommended course guidelines for one major, but not for another. Schools change recommended course "units" based on major on a regular basis. Once you begin to attend the school, you can apply to change majors more easily than to obtain admission. For the vast majority of schools, changing majors is a quick administrative switch by your college guidance counselor. For other schools, it is a short application that is much more easily granted than the original admission to the school.

Part Two: Considering Where to Apply

As you review college websites considering where you would potentially like to attend college and checking the schools' recommended course selections, also check the schools' additional admission guidelines. Print the pages or make a note of each school's grade point average (GPA) and ACT or SAT score range for most admitted freshman students. Also, note whether the school requires any additional admissions tests (such as SAT II Subject Tests, which test individual subject knowledge such as literature or biology). Additional admissions tests are sometimes required by colleges in addition to standard admissions tests. Look around the college or university's website to see if you might like the school, and check the list of majors to see if your goals and talents can flourish at the school.

At this point, do not linger on the school price. When you apply, it is a good idea to apply to two public universities in your state as well as four or so additional colleges and universities that are in-state public schools, out-of-state public schools, or private schools. Compare prices once you receive admissions and financial aid awards to see how much more or

less the various schools will actually cost (sometimes a grant
to attend a private school can keep the price down in an
unexpected way). Some states have made in-state pricing of
public schools much more affordable than going elsewhere.
So, if you live in a state that has excellent in-state pricing for
public schools, and you meet the in-state requirements (which
usually require you to have lived in the state for a certain
length of time), then you might want to apply entirely to in-
state schools.

If it is difficult to think of the schools to which you might
want to apply, check out the most recent magazine college
rankings of schools, and use these as a jumping off point to
help you identify colleges. Then review the school websites.

Part Three: The American College Test (ACT) and

Scholastic Aptitude Test (SAT)

When you have a list of colleges to which you may want to apply and for which you think your grade point average will likely qualify you for admission, then it is time to set a goal timeframe for taking either the ACT or SAT tests. Keep in mind that some schools may also require SAT II Subject Tests or other tests. Most students need only take one test, either the ACT or the SAT.

Choose which test you will take from your notes on your list of schools. Take the test that all of your list of schools will accept. The vast majority of colleges and universities accept both tests. You should set a goal to take either the ACT or SAT in the spring of your junior year or the fall of your senior year. Setting the time to take either test will enable you to create a plan for studying for the test that you have chosen.

Each test is offered several times a year in many testing locations. You must register to take the test about six weeks in advance of the test date. However, you should register well before this registration deadline. Having a set test date will allow you to create a study schedule. The tests cover reading, writing or English, math, and for one test, science subject areas. Both tests have an optional essay component. Check your college selections as you study and gauge whether you should take the essay component. If a college to which you are applying requires the essay be taken, then you must take the optional essay portion of the test. If your essay score will likely help to improve your application, then you should take the essay component, even if it is not required by the school. You will need to gauge your likelihood of success on the essay component through practice and by requesting that someone review your practice essays, such as a tutor, teacher, or parent.

Studying for the ACT or SAT test can be done in a tutoring center or on your own. The benefit of a tutoring center is, first, that you set aside specific blocks of study time that you will stick to (you will not be able to procrastinate, and therefore will apply yourself to the study plan over time.) Second, you will likely take practice tests to gauge whether you feel more comfortable with the ACT or SAT, and then you can decide to take the test on which you think you will do better. Third, you will work with a tutor who knows a great deal about the test and has specifically learned how to teach students ways to succeed on the test. Finally, you will take timed practice tests under accurate test conditions, and these will be graded and reviewed with you. This includes grading of the essay component.

Studying on your own is more difficult to do, but it is certainly possible to succeed by creating a self-study method. Make sure to set aside time to study and do not deviate from your study schedule. Then, obtain study books from the bookstore that contain a guide to the test and many practice questions. Follow those books' instructions for taking timed practice tests. The study books will have example answers or guides to show you why an answer you chose was correct or incorrect on practice test questions. Buy two large study books related to the test you are taking (either the ACT or the SAT) and work through them fully. If you feel that you need help as you are working through your study books, then seek tutoring help. Reaching out to a tutoring service that specializes in preparing students for these tests can be a big help. When your test day draws near, set out everything that you need to take with you to the test the night before, go to sleep early, eat a small breakfast, and arrive early to the testing site.

Another group of standardized college admissions tests that many students take includes English language proficiency tests. These include IELTS, TOEFL, and Pearson Test of English. These are usually taken by international students for whom English is neither a first learned nor primarily used language. Some schools require these tests to confirm proficiency in English as part of their college applications.

Finally, do not forget to check each school to which you may apply to see if it has any additional testing requirements, such as SAT II Subject Tests or any other less often used testing requirement.

Part Four: a Study Refresher

Here are a few study tips to refresh your memory and remind you to recommit to your study plan if you have wavered. Remember, the main component of any study plan is dedicating time to studying. Committing two hours per day every day to studying will increase your grade point average. Therefore, it will increase your success with college admissions.

Start with a table or a desk that is free of clutter. Keep a basket next to the table or desk and when you sit down to study if your desk is not an open, empty space, place anything on top quickly into the basket (a laundry basket will work). This ensures that you always have an uncluttered space to work, and that you do not spend study time cleaning and organizing. Next, make a stack of your course books and notebooks on the desk (take them from your backpack). I like to put the homework that I usually like to do the most at the bottom of the stack and build up to the top of the stack having the homework that I usually like to do the least. If you do this, you will begin with the homework that you like the least, and as the study session continues, it becomes more fun.

A benefit of devoting two hours per day every day is allowing yourself to have a consistent schedule that is easier to plan. This is because studying ahead on nights that you do not have as much allows you to even out the nights that you would ordinarily have too much.

Potentially the best thing to do with extra study time is to review what you have already learned in each course. This is how you study for quizzes and tests in advance. This will certainly increase your course knowledge and grade point average. You will do better on pop quizzes and will avoid cramming for a test in one course while getting behind in another course. Another good option is to work ahead on projects and reports so you will not have to rush before the deadlines.

Discussing assignments early with your teacher (such as, asking if your chosen book will work for the next book report or if your paper topic is satisfactory) will show your teacher that you are committed to your coursework and to getting a good grade in that course. Showing a high level of commitment to your teachers will help you to reach and maintain a higher grade point average.

Finally, do not forget to keep completed course projects to use during the college admissions process. It is a good idea to set aside a few pieces of your best work each year so that you have these when you are looking to provide an example of your writing or another example of your excellent work. Examples of your best work (which you might set aside each year) might include creative and other writing samples, a written translation you did for a language class, or a summary of a science experiment that you performed and for which you kept a record.

Remember, Advanced Placement Courses provide great opportunities to create this work product, and then you have them when you need them during the college admissions process. Written work created in an Advanced Placement Course can be the basis of your college admissions essay. If you write on the topic of a college admissions essay (such as, a specific question asked on the application of one university to which you may apply) for a course project (such as, a course letting you write on a topic of your choice for a writing assignment), then you can use the coursework directly for your college applications. This is one way to involve a teacher in helping to show you the strengths of your essay and to suggest the edits and revisions which you should consider making.

The College Admissions Guidebook

Chapter Four

This chapter will discuss the steps to take in the twelfth grade to secure college admissions. It discusses preparation of your college and university applications and your financial aid application. Correctly demonstrating your hard work in high school thus far on your college applications can help you shine in the eyes of admissions committees.

Part One: the Parts of the College Application

You will be applying to colleges and universities for admission to seek an undergraduate degree (usually a Bachelor of Arts, or a Bachelor of Science degree). Colleges (institutions of higher education granting undergraduate degrees) and universities (institutions of higher education granting both undergraduate degrees and graduate degrees) generally consider the following items as parts of your college application:

- Application form;
- High school transcript (or high school performance report) showing your grades in all subjects;

- Advanced placement exam results;

- Standardized test scores, including the ACT or SAT; and any additional tests required by the school (for example, English proficiency exams or SAT II Tests);

- The essay or personal statement which you write specifically for your college application (this is different than the essay on the ACT or SAT);

- Evaluations and academic recommendations from teachers or others recommending you to the college or university;

- A list of your major extracurricular activities;

- The application fee;

- Unique application parts for specific majors, such as art portfolios or music auditions.

Overall, the applications are a lengthy process, which will require time to complete them all. You will first need to gather the parts of the application and know your target colleges and their application deadlines. Gathering these application items and preparing your essay (personal statement or personal essay) ahead of time will prepare you to fill in the application form with as few delays as possible.

This chapter will discuss the details related to choosing when to apply and how the application process is completed, and then the later part of this chapter will discuss the application for financial aid and how paying for college works.

Part Two: When to Apply and How the Application Process is Completed

Many schools (nearly 700 colleges and universities in 2017) allow application to their schools through "The Common Application." Many schools also allow application on a school specific application form.

The common application is an application for college and university admission, which is designed to simplify the application process by allowing a student to apply to several colleges and universities with a single application. The idea is that completing one application to apply to five or ten schools is easier than completing five or ten individual, school-specific applications and sending one to each school.

As you know from this book, there are many parts for any college application. Applications must include: high school transcripts, Advanced Placement Exam scores, standardized test scores (ACT or SAT, and any other required tests, such as SAT II Tests), an essay (personal statement), recommendations from high school teachers or counselors, answers to questions about extracurricular activities, the application fee, and other unique submissions (such as, portfolios for hopeful art majors or auditions for hopeful music students).

The common application seeks to provide an easier format for your transmission of these various application parts to schools. However, some schools will still request unique application elements. For example, they might have a school-specific essay question. This means that the application for that school will require you to write an additional essay. Another school may have a different unique element. Therefore, the common application will help you to streamline your application process, but there are still portions of the application that are unique to a school and not "common" to all schools. A school may also simply require its own application and not allow the common application. Schools that accept the common application are listed on the common application website.

Start by creating an account on the common application website for your application. Then, find and review the list of "common application member colleges," which are the colleges and universities that allow you to apply to them by using a common application. Reviewing this list and re-visiting school websites is a good way to confirm the choices you are making regarding to which colleges you should apply.

You should apply mostly to schools that:

- Have an academic major (or majors) matching your goals (what you want to study);

- Fit your academic credentials (your grades and test scores match the grades and test scores of students the school most often accepts). It is a good idea to apply to a "safety" school (your grades and test scores exceed the grades and test scores of students the school most often accepts) and a "reach" school (your ideal school to which you might receive admission, but for which your grades and test scores fall somewhat short); and

- Which you would like to attend (you think you would like the school, and it is in a geographic area that you desire);

You should also apply to two schools that:

- Are state schools which would grant in-state tuition to you and which are on par with your grades and standardized test scores. As a note, the vast majority of schools (including out-of-state and private schools) have good possibilities for financial aid. The financial aid element of the decision-making will be discussed at the end of this chapter. Overall, do not let the price tag hold back your applications, but do apply to a couple of in-state schools which would grant lower tuition to you as a state resident.

Once you have confirmed the schools to which you will apply, then it is time to apply. Apply through any application format which you prefer (such as the common application or school-specific application) that the school accepts. Your goal is to successfully complete these applications on time! A completed application is an application that has all parts of the submission completed by you, sent to the school in the required way, and which is received by the school by or before the deadline.

To enter college as a freshman in the fall semester following your spring high school graduation, you will need to apply in the fall or winter of your senior year of high school. Each college has its own deadline for your application, and they generally range from fall to winter (or very early spring) of your senior year of high school. "Rolling admissions" schools accept applications on an ongoing basis, but applications should also be completed during this timeframe (fall and winter of your senior year of high school) because the schools will have a cut-off date for entering freshman fall admissions.

Some colleges and universities offer "early action," "early decision," and "restrictive early action" application deadlines, along with their usual later application deadlines. When using the common application, "early action" involves you sending in your completed application in the fall, usually by November 1st or earlier, based on the school requirements. If you apply as an "early action" candidate because you applied early in the process, you receive an earlier response from the school (either informing you of your admission or declining admission to you). Early action does not require you to commit to attend the school (early action is not binding).

On the common application, "early decision" is also an early application process with you agreeing to attend the school if you are admitted. "Early decision" requires your commitment to attend the school if admitted (early decision is binding).

Also on the common application, "restrictive early action" is a form of early action, where the school places some restrictions on your submission of other early applications.

There are some benefits for applying early with "early action," "early decision," or "restrictive early action" to schools that have these possibilities. For example, some schools are more likely to admit a student who falls a little bit below their standard admission criteria if the student applies on an "early decision" basis. They may extend these somewhat to "early action" and "restrictive early action" applications. Each school has its own criteria for admission on an early basis, so the school can tell you if an early application is likely to benefit you.

Schools that have an especially large number of applicants that year can become more selective as the entering class fills up, so early applicants can, at times, have an easier chance of admission. They are certain that their application will be considered in terms of the schools guidelines, without any issue of an unexpectedly large number of applications.

"Regular decision" and "rolling admissions" deadlines generally require applying in the fall or winter (with some into early spring) of your senior year. This is for consideration for admission to the school to start the next fall. Apply in the fall or winter of your senior year to begin college the fall following your spring high school graduation. Even if a school accepts applications all year long, you need to apply eight or nine months before you wish to start attending the school for many colleges and universities. If you miss the cut-off time for the fall class (or the class is full), even if admitted, you might not be able to start on time.

Now that you know where you would like to apply and when the fully completed application must be submitted, gather the following parts of the application:

- Application form (common application or school-specific application forms);

- High school transcript (high school performance report) showing your grades in all subjects (on the common application also look for the term "school report," which is a form you request from your counselor to which the counselor can directly attach a transcript);

- Advanced Placement Exam results;

- Standardized test scores, including the ACT or SAT and any additional tests the school requires (such as SAT II Subject Matter Tests, or English proficiency exams);

- The essay or personal statement which you write specifically for your college application (this is different than the essay on the ACT or SAT);

- Evaluations and academic recommendations from teachers or others recommending you to the college or university;

- A list of your major extracurricular activities;

- The application fee;

- Unique application parts for specific majors, such as art portfolios or music auditions.

Next, fill in the common application (or school-specific application) form. Make sure that your application form is completely filled in, that all of the information that you have provided is accurate, and that there are no misspellings.

You should treat every single answer on the application with the care that you would provide to a lengthy, formal essay submission. For example, if you write a paragraph about extracurricular activities for an application submission, I suggest that you initially prepare it on a word document. Print it, check it over, and have another person (such as a parent or teacher) proofread all such paragraphs, and then electronically copy the paragraphs onto your online application. It is helpful to keep a separate word document housing all of your application answers that involve more than a sentence or two. This helps with proofreading and loss of electronic information issues and allows you to use these answers again on any later school-specific applications.

The common application will require an essay, which is called a "personal statement" or "personal essay." School-specific applications will also require an essay. Some schools will require additional written questions be answered. These are called "college-specific questions," "member questions," or "writing supplements" on the common application. If a "writing supplement" must be submitted later, make a note and do not forget to do it. It is helpful to have a parent also keeping track of deadlines with you. Set up a reminder in advance of the deadline, just in case you forget.

Remember, it is important to prepare each written essay and answer in a word document and print it. Carefully check it and have a parent or teacher proofread it for mistakes (such as misspellings). Then, electronically copy it into your application once it reflects your best work. Keep the word document, and use your essays and answers again for other schools' applications if the questions asked by the schools are the same.

Make sure to remove all school-specific information in your essay if it is going to several schools. Do not apply to the University of Michigan with an application essay that says how much you would like to attend Ohio State University. That kind of mistake can cost you your admission.

The remaining portions of the application are documents reflecting your past work over the course of your time in high school. You will need to obtain these for inclusion on your application. You will also need to request that some of these documents be sent from your school, or a testing company, directly to the colleges or universities to which you are applying. Follow the specific application instructions for inputting or sending this information.

Part Three: the Application for Financial Aid

To apply for financial aid, first, complete a "Free Application for Federal Student Aid." This is usually referred to by its acronym "FAFSA." The FAFSA is a financial application, which you will find online. You will create an account, and fill in the application by providing personal information, such as your birthday, address, and social security number, and the personal financial information of you and your parents.

The FAFSA will also request that you fill in the names of the colleges and universities to which you have applied or may apply. You can put in the likely schools or return to the FAFSA to add additional schools as you determine the schools to which you will apply. The FAFSA is a federal government application, which will also link in your home state financial aid applications that you should fill in as well. Some states just use the FAFSA form for determining financial aid. The FAFSA is the central form used to determine the financial aid, which you can receive, including federal, state, and college or university-based aid. Make sure to check with your guidance counselor for additional state financial aid forms if the FAFSA does not inform you of them.

The types of financial aid generally include grants, loans, and work-study (student on campus job) eligibility. You can also apply directly to the college or university for scholarships; these are listed on the schools' websites. Read the school website for programs in which the school might participate that help pay for college, such as The Reserve Officers' Training Corps (ROTC), which is an armed forces college-based training program. ROTC trains future commissioned officers of the United States Armed Forces on college campuses and can pay for part (or sometimes all) of participating college or university tuition.

The FAFSA application is your main financial aid application, along with any state forms (which will usually be linked to the FAFSA). However, check with your guidance counselor for additional state forms if the FAFSA does not inform you of them, and perform some web searches for your state name and state financial aid forms (or look for your state grant agency). Secondarily, the individual school websites list scholarships and programs that can lead you to additional sources of financial aid information. A third possibility is to search for scholarships elsewhere through web searching. After completing your college applications, the FAFSA, and any state financial aid forms, and applying directly to the school for scholarships listed on their website, you may or may not want to undertake this type of additional searching. It is simply far less likely to pay off, so just make sure you do the FAFSA, state forms, and school website searches before you do any other steps.

The necessary steps are: applying to the schools, completing the FAFSA (along with any additional state forms), and a thorough review of your potential colleges' websites. Beyond this, you can gauge the value of spending time searching the internet, and whether it will likely lead you to a financially beneficial result.

Let us break down the process and the result in greater detail. Do the FAFSA (the most important financial aid application) around the time of your college applications. You will want to complete the FAFSA in the fall or winter of your senior year of high school. Do not wait! Double-check your state by asking your guidance counselor and web searching for state-based grant money from your home state. Next, apply to the college or university directly for scholarships listed on the school's website based on the application date for each listed scholarship for which you might be considered. The school website will also inform you of any programs in which the school participates, such as ROTC.

Part Four: How Paying for College Works

Now that you know how to apply, here is how the money works. Every college or university has a "cost of attendance" number reflecting the full cost for you to take full-time courses, live in a dormitory, and eat on campus. The goal of the FAFSA process (which is created by the federal government) is to enable you to attend the college you choose by helping you and your family to meet the school's "cost of attendance." By completing the FAFSA application (and any state aid applications), you provide the information necessary for provision of grant and loan money to help you with this "cost of attendance." After you have successfully applied to colleges, you will receive your admission letter or email, and (if admitted) a later letter or email showing your financial aid package. The financial aid package shows how the school's financial aid counselors have used your FAFSA application, any state financial aid forms, and any school scholarship applications, to meet the "cost of attendance" number to enable you to attend that school.

You will see the cost for taking courses, living in the dormitory, and eating on campus, along with the financial aid available to you and your parents to meet this cost, and the amount that your family can likely contribute or borrow. Most often loans are available to meet the expected family contribution portion of the financial aid package.

The financial aid awarded includes grants, loans, and work-study employment. You can also apply to the school for scholarships or other programs (such as schools with ROTC on campus, for which you would apply to both the school and the military) under those specific deadlines.

A "grant" is money provided to the student from the government, which the student does not have to repay. This is sometimes called "free money" because it is a grant of money (a gift), not a loan. Grants are awarded to students with more financial need ("need-based financial aid"). If you are awarded a grant, it is paid directly to the school after you enroll and a bill is created. The bill will show the cost for school minus this grant money (with the appropriate amount allocated to the applicable semester) as a payment made on your behalf from the government to the school. You never have to repay money given by a grant.

"Loans" are for students and/or their parents. A loan is money you or your parents may borrow (and later repay) to pay now for college. You will fill out additional loan paperwork (including a promissory note, which means that you promise to repay) and entrance counseling paperwork (showing you have read and understand how the loan works). A loan is money that you and/or your parents must repay to the company lending the money to you to pay for college.

"Work-study" is eligibility for employment that can help you work on campus and earn money. You seek out and apply on campus for a variety of part-time jobs (such as, assisting in a campus office or shop), and receive money in the form of a paycheck, just as you would for a regular part-time job. You can use the money as you normally would use money from a part-time job for expenses and fun. Eligibility for work-study employment helps you to find work on campus because some campus jobs are set aside for those who have work-study eligibility.

A scholarship is money provided by the school to you on a "merit and need-based" or purely "merit-based" basis. Scholarships provided to students under merit and need-based criterions are awarded to students with greater financial need, who have achievements that qualify them for the scholarship. These students win the scholarships because each scholarship winner has the required achievement and has met the financial need criterion for eligibility for the award. The best students who also meet need-based requirements win the scholarship.

Purely merit-based scholarships are won by students with the best achievements in the required category for that scholarship, such as, outstanding academic achievement (high school grade point average) outstanding student entering as a biology major (or other major), outstanding entering musician to the school of music, etc.

Available scholarships can be found on the school website, and you apply for them based on their instructions. Scholarship winnings (the money provided by the scholarships) are often applied directly to your school bill, showing an amount paid on your behalf to lower the school bill. Scholarships do not have to be repaid; they are so called "free money."

The FAFSA must be completed every year of college in the winter before the following school year. You should also double check your state forms (usually linked to by the FAFSA) and also revisit your school website each year for scholarship opportunities available to sophomore, junior, and senior college students as well as for summer opportunities for which funding is available.

Part Five: Make Your Decision!

Lastly, it is time to make a decision! Do a final comparison of the colleges and universities to which you are admitted, and compare the aid offered in the school financial aid packages. Once you have chosen your school, send back your agreement to attend your chosen college or university on time, and send back your financial aid agreement. Now that a school has chosen you, do not forget to choose the school too!

The College Admissions Workbook

HIGH SCHOOL GRADUATION REQUIREMENTS

Chart of My High School Graduation Requirements:

The number of courses I must take to graduate

In four years, I need to complete _____ classes, and/or

_____ credits to graduate. (You can find this number in the

course guidebook or obtain it from your guidance counselor.)

This means that I need to complete _____ classes per

year, which is _____classes per semester.

My Course Requirements and Electives

Use your high school course guidebook (or list of

graduation requirements) to fill in the chart starting on the next

page. You can obtain the course guidebook or list of

graduation requirements from your guidance counselor. Also,

have your guidance counselor check that you have not made

any mistakes once you finish your chart.

My Course Requirements and Electives

MATH

_____ math classes (the number of math classes your high school requires) listed in the order in which you must take them.

One must be _____ (name of required course)

One must be _____ (name of required course)

One must be _____ (name of required course)

One must be _____ (name of required course)

One must be _____ (name of required course)

One must be _____ (name of required course)

One must be _____ (name of required course)

One must be _____ (name of required course)

I may choose additional math courses listed on the high school math course list. These must be taken in order (for example, Algebra II may only be allowed after Algebra I).

One can be _____ (name of additional course)

One can be _____ (name of additional course)

One can be _____ (name of additional course)

One can be _____ (name of additional course)

One can be _____ (name of additional course)

One can be _____ (name of additional course)

One can be _____ (name of additional course)

One can be _____ (name of additional course)

SCIENCE

_____ science classes (the number of science classes your high school requires) listed in the order in which you must take them.

One must be _____ (name of required course)

One must be _____ (name of required course)

One must be _____ (name of required course)

One must be _____ (name of required course)

One must be _____ (name of required course)

One must be _____ (name of required course)

One must be _____ (name of required course)

One must be _____ (name of required course)

I may choose additional science courses from the science courses listed on the high school science course list. Note that some science courses have a prerequisite; for example, biochemistry may only be allowed after chemistry is completed in your school (chemistry would be the prerequisite for biochemistry).

One can be _____ (name of additional course)

One can be _____ (name of additional course)

One can be _____ (name of additional course)

One can be _____ (name of additional course)

One can be _____ (name of additional course)

One can be _____ (name of additional course)

One can be _____ (name of additional course)

LANGUAGE ARTS (ENGLISH)

_____ language arts classes (the number of language arts classes your high school requires) listed in the order in which you must take them.

One must be _____ (name of required course)

One must be _____ (name of required course)

One must be _____ (name of required course)

One must be _____ (name of required course)

One must be _____ (name of required course)

One must be _____ (name of required course)

One must be _____ (name of required course)

One must be _____ (name of required course)

I may choose additional courses from the language arts courses listed on the high school language arts course list (make a note of any prerequisites).

One can be _____ (name of additional course)

One can be _____ (name of additional course)

One can be _____ (name of additional course)

One can be _____ (name of additional course)

One can be _____ (name of additional course)

One can be _____ (name of additional course)

One can be _____ (name of additional course)

One can be _____ (name of additional course)

SOCIAL STUDIES (HISTORY)

_____ social studies classes (the number of social studies classes your high school requires) listed in the order in which you must take them.

    One must be _____ (name of required course)

    One must be _____ (name of required course)

    One must be _____ (name of required course)

    One must be _____ (name of required course)

    One must be _____ (name of required course)

    One must be _____ (name of required course)

    One must be _____ (name of required course)

    One must be _____ (name of required course)

I may choose additional courses from the social studies courses listed on the high school social studies course list (note any with prerequisites).

One can be _____ (name of additional course)

One can be _____ (name of additional course)

One can be _____ (name of additional course)

One can be _____ (name of additional course)

One can be _____ (name of additional course)

One can be _____ (name of additional course)

One can be _____ (name of additional course)

One can be _____ (name of additional course)

FOREIGN LANGUAGE

_____ foreign language classes (the number of foreign

language classes your high school requires) listed in the order

in which you must take them.

The first foreign language I choose to learn to fulfill the

requirement

One must be _____ (name of

required course)

One must be _____ (name of

required course)

One must be _____ (name of

required course)

One must be _____ (name of

required course)

One must be _____ (name of

required course)

One must be _____ (name of

required course)

One must be _____ (name of

required course)

I may choose additional foreign language courses from the foreign language courses listed on the high school course list. Note that these will have specific prerequisites, so list them in the order in which you must take them.

The second foreign language I choose to learn (if this is where my talents lie)

One can be _____ (name of additional course)

One can be _____ (name of additional course)

One can be _____ (name of additional course)

One can be _____ (name of additional course)

One can be _____ (name of additional course)

One can be _____ (name of additional course)

One can be _____ (name of additional course)

OTHER REQUIRED COURSES

_____ additionally required courses such as health, physical education, art, music, and any others. This is the number of additionally required courses at your high school (outside of the main academic areas). List the courses in the order in which you must take them (if there is an order).

One must be _____ (name of required course)

One must be _____ (name of required course)

One must be _____ (name of required course)

One must be _____ (name of required course)

One must be _____ (name of required course)

One must be _____ (name of required course)

One must be _____ (name of required course)

ELECTIVE COURSES

List the elective courses which you plan to take in addition to your selections in the five main subject areas and in addition to the school's additional course requirements. Concentrate on taking courses for any area of special interest which you may decide to pursue in college (such as orchestra, band, theater, or fine arts).

One can be _____ (name of additional course)

One can be _____ (name of additional course)

One can be _____ (name of additional course)

One can be _____ (name of additional course)

One can be _____ (name of additional course)

One can be _____ (name of additional course)

One can be _____ (name of additional course)

One can be _____ (name of

additional course)

One can be _____ (name of

additional course)

One can be _____ (name of

additional course)

One can be _____ (name of

additional course)

One can be _____ (name of

additional course)

One can be _____ (name of

additional course)

One can be _____ (name of

additional course)

One can be _____ (name of

additional course)

One can be _____ (name of

additional course)

COURSEPLAN

Create and Chart the Courses You Will Take:

This is a chart for creating a course selection plan based on your high school graduation requirements and your talents. Several copies are provided for you to revise your plan over time.

For the ninth grade, fill in the course you will take in each listed subject area that will fulfill a graduation requirement.

Ninth Grade Fall Semester

Math

Science

Language arts

Social studies

Foreign language

Sixth course

Seventh course (provided your school has a seventh period)

Ninth Grade Spring Semester

Math

Science

Language arts

Social studies

Foreign language

Sixth course

Seventh course (provided your school has a seventh period)

For the tenth grade, fill in the course you will take in each listed subject area that will fulfill a graduation requirement and for academic subjects in which your talents lie (after your graduation requirements are fulfilled).

Tenth Grade Fall Semester

Math

Science

Language arts

Social studies

Foreign language

Sixth course

Seventh course (provided your school has a seventh period)

Tenth Grade Spring Semester

Math

Science

Language arts

Social studies

Foreign language

Sixth course

Seventh course (provided your school has a seventh period)

For the eleventh grade, fill in the course you will take in each listed subject area that will fulfill a graduation requirement and for academic subjects in which your talents lie (after your graduation requirements are fulfilled). Also, confirm that you fulfill the "unit" recommendations of colleges and universities to which you will likely apply.

Eleventh Grade Fall Semester

Math
Or other academic subject

Science
Or other academic subject

Language arts
Or other academic subject

Social studies
Or other academic subject

Foreign language
Or other academic subject

Sixth course

Seventh course (provided your school has a seventh period)

Eleventh Grade Spring Semester

Math
Or other academic subject

Science
Or other academic subject

Language arts
Or other academic subject

Social studies
Or other academic subject

Foreign language
Or other academic subject

Sixth course

Seventh course (provided your school has a seventh period)

For the twelfth grade, fill in the course you will take in each listed subject area that will fulfill a graduation requirement and for academic subjects in which your talents lie (after your graduation requirements are fulfilled). Also, confirm that you fulfill the "unit" recommendations of colleges and universities to which you will likely apply.

Twelfth Grade Fall Semester

Math
Or other academic subject

Science
Or other academic subject

Language arts
Or other academic subject

Social studies
Or other academic subject

Foreign language
Or other academic subject

Sixth course

Seventh course (provided your school has a seventh period)

Twelfth Grade Spring Semester

Math
Or other academic subject

Science
Or other academic subject

Language arts
Or other academic subject

Social studies

Or other academic subject

Foreign language
Or other academic subject

Sixth course

Seventh course (provided your school has a seventh period)

Revise Your Course Plan

For the ninth grade, fill in the course you will take in each listed subject area that will fulfill a graduation requirement.

Ninth Grade Fall Semester

Math

Science

Language arts

Social studies

Foreign language

Sixth course

Seventh course (provided your school has a seventh period)

Ninth Grade Spring Semester

Math

Science

Language arts

Social studies

Foreign language

Sixth course

Seventh course (provided your school has a seventh period)

For the tenth grade, fill in the course you will take in each listed subject area that will fulfill a graduation requirement and for academic subjects in which your talents lie (after your graduation requirements are fulfilled).

Tenth Grade Fall Semester

Math

Science

Language arts

Social studies

Foreign language

Sixth course

Seventh course (provided your school has a seventh period)

Tenth Grade Spring Semester

Math

Science

Language arts

Social studies

Foreign language

Sixth course

Seventh course (provided your school has a seventh period)

For the eleventh grade, fill in the course you will take in each listed subject area that will fulfill a graduation requirement and for academic subjects in which your talents lie (after your graduation requirements are fulfilled). Also, confirm that you fulfill the "unit" recommendations of colleges and universities to which you will likely apply.

Eleventh Grade Fall Semester

Math
Or other academic subject

Science
Or other academic subject

Language arts
Or other academic subject

Social studies
Or other academic subject

Foreign language
Or other academic subject

Sixth course

Seventh course (provided your school has a seventh period)

Eleventh Grade Spring Semester

Math
Or other academic subject

Science
Or other academic subject

Language arts
Or other academic subject

Social studies
Or other academic subject

Foreign language
Or other academic subject

Sixth course

Seventh course (provided your school has a seventh period)

For the twelfth grade, fill in the course you will take in each listed subject area that will fulfill a graduation requirement and for academic subjects in which your talents lie (after your graduation requirements are fulfilled). Also, confirm that you fulfill the "unit" recommendations of colleges and universities to which you will likely apply.

Twelfth Grade Fall Semester

Math
Or other academic subject

Science
Or other academic subject

Language arts
Or other academic subject

Social studies
Or other academic subject

Foreign language
Or other academic subject

Sixth course

Seventh course (provided your school has a seventh period)

Twelfth Grade Spring Semester

Math
Or other academic subject

Science
Or other academic subject

Language arts
Or other academic subject

Social studies

Or other academic subject

Foreign language
Or other academic subject

Sixth course

Seventh course (provided your school has a seventh period)

Revise Your Course Plan

For the ninth grade, fill in the course you will take in each listed subject area that will fulfill a graduation requirement.

Ninth Grade Fall Semester

Math

Science

Language arts

Social studies

Foreign language

Sixth course

Seventh course (provided your school has a seventh period)

Ninth Grade Spring Semester

Math

Science

Language arts

Social studies

Foreign language

Sixth course

Seventh course (provided your school has a seventh period)

For the tenth grade, fill in the course you will take in each listed subject area that will fulfill a graduation requirement and for academic subjects in which your talents lie (after your graduation requirements are fulfilled).

Tenth Grade Fall Semester

Math

Science

Language arts

Social studies

Foreign language

Sixth course

Seventh course (provided your school has a seventh period)

Tenth Grade Spring Semester

Math

Science

Language arts

Social studies

Foreign language

Sixth course

Seventh course (provided your school has a seventh period)

For the eleventh grade, fill in the course you will take in each listed subject area that will fulfill a graduation requirement and for academic subjects in which your talents lie (after your graduation requirements are fulfilled). Also, confirm that you fulfill the
"unit" recommendations of colleges and universities to which you will likely apply.

Eleventh Grade Fall Semester

Math
Or other academic subject

Science
Or other academic subject

Language arts
Or other academic subject

Social studies
Or other academic subject

Foreign language
Or other academic subject

Sixth course

Seventh course (provided your school has a seventh period)

Eleventh Grade Spring Semester

Math
Or other academic subject

Science
Or other academic subject

Language arts
Or other academic subject

Social studies

Or other academic subject

Foreign language
Or other academic subject

Sixth course

Seventh course (provided your school has a seventh period)

For the twelfth grade, fill in the course you will take in each listed subject area that will fulfill a graduation requirement and for academic subjects in which your talents lie (after your graduation requirements are fulfilled). Also, confirm that you fulfill the "unit" recommendations of colleges and universities to which you will likely apply.

Twelfth Grade Fall Semester

Math
Or other academic subject

Science
Or other academic subject

Language arts
Or other academic subject

Social studies
Or other academic subject

Foreign language
Or other academic subject

Sixth course

Seventh course (provided your school has a seventh period)

Twelfth Grade Spring Semester

Math
Or other academic subject

Science
Or other academic subject

Language arts
Or other academic subject

Social studies
Or other academic subject

Foreign language
Or other academic subject

Sixth course

Seventh course (provided your school has a seventh period)

Revise Your Course Plan

For the ninth grade, fill in the course you will take in each listed subject area that will fulfill a graduation requirement.

Ninth Grade Fall Semester

Math

Science

Language arts

Social studies

Foreign language

Sixth course

Seventh course (provided your school has a seventh period)

Ninth Grade Spring Semester

Math

Science

Language arts

Social studies

Foreign language

Sixth course

Seventh course (provided your school has a seventh period)

For the tenth grade, fill in the course you will take in each listed subject area that will fulfill a graduation requirement and for academic subjects in which your talents lie (after your graduation requirements are fulfilled).

Tenth Grade Fall Semester

Math

Science

Language arts

Social studies

Foreign language

Sixth course

Seventh course (provided your school has a seventh period)

Tenth Grade Spring Semester

Math

Science

Language arts

Social studies

Foreign language

Sixth course

Seventh course (provided your school has a seventh period)

For the eleventh grade, fill in the course you will take in each listed subject area that will fulfill a graduation requirement and for academic subjects in which your talents lie (after your graduation requirements are fulfilled). Also, confirm that you fulfill the "unit" recommendations of colleges and universities to which you will likely apply.

Eleventh Grade Fall Semester

Math
Or other academic subject

Science
Or other academic subject

Language arts
Or other academic subject

Social studies
Or other academic subject

Foreign language
Or other academic subject

Sixth course

Seventh course (provided your school has a seventh period)

Eleventh Grade Spring Semester

Math
Or other academic subject

Science
Or other academic subject

Language arts
Or other academic subject

Social studies
Or other academic subject

Foreign language
Or other academic subject

Sixth course

Seventh course (provided your school has a seventh period)

For the twelfth grade, fill in the course you will take in each listed subject area that will fulfill a graduation requirement and for academic subjects in which your talents lie (after your graduation requirements are fulfilled). Also, confirm that you fulfill the 'unit' recommendations of colleges and universities to which you will likely apply.

Twelfth Grade Fall Semester

Math
Or other academic subject

Science
Or other academic subject

Language arts
Or other academic subject

Social studies
Or other academic subject

Foreign language
Or other academic subject

Sixth course

Seventh course (provided your school has a seventh period)

Twelfth Grade Spring Semester

Math
Or other academic subject

Science
Or other academic subject

Language arts
Or other academic subject

Social studies
Or other academic subject

Foreign language
Or other academic subject

Sixth course

Seventh course (provided your school has a seventh period)

Revise Your Course Plan

For the ninth grade, fill in the course you will take in each listed subject area that will fulfill a graduation requirement.

Ninth Grade Fall Semester

Math

Science

Language arts

Social studies

Foreign language

Sixth course

Seventh course (provided your school has a seventh period)

Ninth Grade Spring Semester

Math

Science

Language arts

Social studies

Foreign language

Sixth course

Seventh course (provided your school has a seventh period)

For the tenth grade, fill in the course you will take in each listed subject area that will fulfill a graduation requirement and for academic subjects in which your talents lie (after your graduation requirements are fulfilled).

Tenth Grade Fall Semester

Math

Science

Language arts

Social studies

Foreign language

Sixth course

Seventh course (provided your school has a seventh period)

Tenth Grade Spring Semester

Math

Science

Language arts

Social studies

Foreign language

Sixth course

Seventh course (provided your school has a seventh period)

For the eleventh grade, fill in the course you will take in each listed subject area that will fulfill a graduation requirement and for academic subjects in which your talents lie (after your graduation requirements are fulfilled). Also, confirm that you fulfill the "unit" recommendations of colleges and universities to which you will likely apply.

Eleventh Grade Fall Semester

Math
Or other academic subject

Science
Or other academic subject

Language arts
Or other academic subject

Social studies
Or other academic subject

Foreign language
Or other academic subject

Sixth course

Seventh course (provided your school has a seventh period)

Eleventh Grade Spring Semester

Math
Or other academic subject

Science
Or other academic subject

Language arts
Or other academic subject

Social studies
Or other academic subject

Foreign language
Or other academic subject

Sixth course

Seventh course (provided your school has a seventh period)

For the twelfth grade, fill in the course you will take in each listed subject area that will fulfill a graduation requirement and for academic subjects in which your talents lie (after your graduation requirements are fulfilled). Also, confirm that you fulfill the 'unit' recommendations of colleges and universities to which you will likely apply.

Twelfth Grade Fall Semester

Math
Or other academic subject

Science
Or other academic subject

Language arts
Or other academic subject

Social studies
Or other academic subject

Foreign language
Or other academic subject

Sixth course

Seventh course (provided your school has a seventh period)

Twelfth Grade Spring Semester

Math
Or other academic subject

Science
Or other academic subject

Language arts
Or other academic subject

Social studies
Or other academic subject

Foreign language
Or other academic subject

Sixth course

Seventh course (provided your school has a seventh period)

MEETING YOUR GOALS BY CREATING A STUDY PLAN

My goals for the ninth grade are:

-
-
-
-
-
-
-
-
-
-
-
-
-
-
-

My study plan for the ninth grade involves these things:

-
-
-
-
-
-
-
-
-
-
-
-
-
-
-
-

MEETING YOUR GOALS BY CREATING A STUDY PLAN

My goals for the tenth grade are:

-
-
-
-
-
-
-
-
-
-
-
-
-
-
-

My study plan for the tenth grade involves these things:

-
-
-
-
-
-
-
-
-
-
-
-
-
-
-

MEETING YOUR GOALS BY CREATING A STUDY PLAN

My goals for the eleventh grade are:

-
-
-
-
-
-
-
-
-
-
-
-
-
-
-

My study plan for the eleventh grade involves these things:

-
-
-
-
-
-
-
-
-
-
-
-
-
-
-
-

MEETING YOUR GOALS BY CREATING A STUDY PLAN

My goals for the twelfth grade are:

-
-
-
-
-
-
-
-
-
-
-
-
-
-
-

My study plan for the twelfth grade involves these things:

-

-

-

-

-

-

-

-

-

-

-

-

-

-

-

-

CHOOSING YOUR COLLEGES AND UNIVERSITIES

Ideas for Creating Your List of Colleges to Which to Apply

You should apply mostly to schools that:

- Have an academic major (or majors) matching your goals (what you want to study);

- Fit your academic credentials (your grades and test scores match the grades and test scores of students the school most often accepts). It is a good idea to apply to a "safety" school (your grades and test scores exceed the grades and test scores of students the school most often accepts) and a "reach" school (your ideal school to which you might receive admission, but for which your grades and test scores fall somewhat short); and

- Which you would like to attend (you think you would like the school, and it is in a geographic area that you desire);

You should also apply to two schools that:

- Are state schools which would grant in-state tuition to you and which are on par with your grades and standardized test scores. As a note, the vast majority

of schools (including out-of-state and private schools)

have good possibilities for financial aid. Overall, do not

let the price tag hold back your applications, but do

apply to a couple of in-state schools that would grant

lower tuition to you as a state resident.

A List of Notes about a School

Notes about _____

-
-
-
-
-
-
-
-
-
-
-
-
-
-

A List of Notes about a School

Notes about _____

-
-
-
-
-
-
-
-
-
-
-
-
-
-

A List of Notes about a School

Notes about _____

-
-
-
-
-
-
-
-
-
-
-
-
-
-

A List of Notes about a School

Notes about _____

-
-
-
-
-
-
-
-
-
-
-
-
-
-

A List of Notes about a School

Notes about _____

-

-

-

-

-

-

-

-

-

-

-

-

-

-

A List of Notes about a School

Notes about _____

-
-
-
-
-
-
-
-
-
-
-
-
-
-

A List of Notes about a School

Notes about _____

-
-
-
-
-
-
-
-
-
-
-
-
-
-

A List of Notes about a School

Notes about _____

-
-
-
-
-
-
-
-
-
-
-
-
-
-

A List of Notes about a School

Notes about _____

-
-
-
-
-
-
-
-
-
-
-
-
-
-

A List of Notes about a School

Notes about _____

-
-
-
-
-
-
-
-
-
-
-
-
-
-

APPLYING TO SCHOOLS

A List of the Parts of the College Application

You will need to gather the following parts of the application to successfully apply to most schools. The following are pages for you to use to chart dates, deadlines, and notes.

- Application form (common application, or school - specific application forms);

- High school transcript (high school performance report) showing your grades in all subjects (on the common application also look for the term "school report," which is a form you request from your counselor to which the counselor can directly attach a transcript);

- Advanced Placement Exam results;

- Standardized test scores, including the ACT or SAT and any additional tests the school requires (such as SAT II Subject Matter Tests, or English proficiency exams);

- The essay or personal statement which you write specifically for your college application (this is different than the essay on the ACT or SAT);

- Evaluations and academic recommendations from teachers or others recommending you to the college or university;

- A list of your major extracurricular activities;

- The application fee;

- Unique application parts for specific majors, such as art portfolios or music auditions.

A List of Dates and Deadlines for My College Application

To _____

1.

2.

3.

4.

5.

6.

7.

8.

9.

10.

11.

12.

13.

14.

15.

A List of Notes for My College Application

To _____

1.

2.

3.

4.

5.

6.

7.

8.

9.

10.

11.

12.

13.

14.

15.

A List of Dates and Deadlines for My College Application

To _____

1.

2.

3.

4.

5.

6.

7.

8.

9.

10.

11.

12.

13.

14.

15.

A List of Notes for My College Application

To _____

1.

2.

3.

4.

5.

6.

7.

8.

9.

10.

11.

12.

13.

14.

15.

A List of Dates and Deadlines for My College Application

To _____

1.

2.

3.

4.

5.

6.

7.

8.

9.

10.

11.

12.

13.

14.

15.

A List of Notes for My College Application

To _____

1.

2.

3.

4.

5.

6.

7.

8.

9.

10.

11.

12.

13.

14.

15.

A List of Dates and Deadlines for My College Application

To _____

1.

2.

3.

4.

5.

6.

7.

8.

9.

10.

11.

12.

13.

14.

15.

A List of Notes for My College Application

To _____

1.

2.

3.

4.

5.

6.

7.

8.

9.

10.

11.

12.

13.

14.

15.

A List of Dates and Deadlines for My College Application

To _____

1.

2.

3.

4.

5.

6.

7.

8.

9.

10.

11.

12.

13.

14.

15.

A List of Notes for My College Application

To _____

1.

2.

3.

4.

5.

6.

7.

8.

9.

10.

11.

12.

13.

14.

15.

A List of Dates and Deadlines for My College Application

To _____

1.

2.

3.

4.

5.

6.

7.

8.

9.

10.

11.

12.

13.

14.

15.

A List of Notes for My College Application

To _____

1.

2.

3.

4.

5.

6.

7.

8.

9.

10.

11.

12.

13.

14.

15.

A List of Dates and Deadlines for My College Application

To _____

1.

2.

3.

4.

5.

6.

7.

8.

9.

10.

11.

12.

13.

14.

15.

A List of Notes for My College Application

To _____

1.

2.

3.

4.

5.

6.

7.

8.

9.

10.

11.

12.

13.

14.

15.

A List of Dates and Deadlines for My College Application

To _____

1.

2.

3.

4.

5.

6.

7.

8.

9.

10.

11.

12.

13.

14.

15.

A List of Notes for My College Application

To _____

1.

2.

3.

4.

5.

6.

7.

8.

9.

10.

11.

12.

13.

14.

15.

A List of Dates and Deadlines for My College Application

To _____

1.

2.

3.

4.

5.

6.

7.

8.

9.

10.

11.

12.

13.

14.

15.

A List of Notes for My College Application

To _____

1.

2.

3.

4.

5.

6.

7.

8.

9.

10.

11.

12.

13.

14.

15.

A List of Dates and Deadlines for My College Application

To _____

1.

2.

3.

4.

5.

6.

7.

8.

9.

10.

11.

12.

13.

14.

15.

A List of Notes for My College Application

To _____

1.

2.

3.

4.

5.

6.

7.

8.

9.

10.

11.

12.

13.

14.

15.

APPLYING FOR FINANCIAL AID

A List of Notes about My Financial Aid Applications

(dates, deadlines, and ideas)

-
-
-
-
-
-
-
-
-
-
-
-
-
-
-

A List of Notes about My Financial Aid Applications

(dates, deadlines, and ideas)

-
-
-
-
-
-
-
-
-
-
-
-
-
-
-

A List of Notes about My Financial Aid Applications

(dates, deadlines, and ideas)

-
-
-
-
-
-
-
-
-
-
-
-
-
-
-

A List of Notes about My Financial Aid Applications

(dates, deadlines, and ideas)

-
-
-
-
-
-
-
-
-
-
-
-
-
-
-

A List of Notes about My Financial Aid Applications

(dates, deadlines, and ideas)

-
-
-
-
-
-
-
-
-
-
-
-
-
-
-

Made in the USA
Middletown, DE
05 July 2017